at fifty

a poem

at fifty

a poem

joel oppenheimer

1982
saint andrews press
laurinburg, north carolina

ISBN 0-932662-39-0

Library of Congress No. 82-061230

this poem was written with the help
of a generous grant from the national
endowment for the arts.

811

contents

contents concluded

at fifty

a poem

Loving means not letting immediacy wither
under the omnipresent weight of mediation and economics,
and in such fidelity it becomes itself mediated,
as a stubborn counterpressure.

He alone loves who has the strength
to hold fast to love . . . .

It is the test of feeling
whether it goes beyond feeling through permanence . . . .

The love which in the guise of unreflecting spontaneity,
and proud of its alleged integrity,
relies exclusively on what it takes to be
the voice of the heart, and runs away as soon as
it no longer thinks it can hear that voice,
is in this supreme independence precisely the tool of society . . . .

The fidelity exacted by society is a means of unfreedom,
but only through fidelity can freedom
achieve insubordination to society's command.

from Minima Moralia/Theodor Adorno

I

necessarily
the goddess is
unattainable
> *nympholepsy*
> that rapture attained
> straining for the
> unattainable
and the stroking
touches only surface

yet it causes her
to rise near those surfaces

the evidence is in
the sounds

II

written:
i felt desire
but wanted love

to another:
which is not to say
i won't try to
seduce you archaic
notion to make us
laugh together

to another:
a partly empty bed
awaits you
          sadly
this brought her here

to another:
no! no! no! no! no!
to another:
yes and yes and yes

III

waking middle night
walking the hall
smell of pine-sol
one smell and back now
shades of proust
whirling back
eight years old
annie the cleaning lady
across from me at lunch

soup sucked straight up
from saucer poured from bowl
clothes layer on layer
smell slightly stale and sour
smell of cleaning cleaning

old fat ugly an anomaly
this woman spends her life
cleaning other people's houses

cooled the soup in the saucer
and her coffee also

then swung back further
three or four years old
sharing the room with
anna the young strong
depression girl hired
to help sick mother
tend little boy and house
me and anna at the church
at mount st vincent feeding
the goldfish in the pool
outside it then inside
curled in corner of
a pew while anna prayed
and made confession

one night in bed but not asleep
watched anna slide from dress
stand in slip readying to go out
first woman i saw undressed
natural my eve my astarte

anna young going out
with bill the cop she married
and smelled different
and was desirable and formed
my image of a woman

IV

the blouse was
sequined it
caught the hand

anything for
beauty she said

reaching through
the neck fondled
her breast nipples
filled my hand
i love them

i think you love
women she said

may just have been
right or perhaps
it is only nipples

V

i did ask if
you'd marry me
the first time
we met but that
was for ulterior
motives the things
you owned and had
in storage three
hand presses and
a lot of type
unable to ask
for heavier things
thinking you were
already incumbered

in response to
my query about
unincumbered
the editor said
perhaps it isn't
le mot juste
for referring to
the state of being
unmarried
but your letter says
you are unincumbered

so marry me

VI

oh rachel
             your
wide shoulders
                  your
small breasts surprised
me so as the
blouse fell from
your back

VII

not only beautiful
but also willing in addition
to read two year's worth
of an obscure trade journal
to find me a copy
of an early publication
a note on why j and u
appear as they do
in the type case
not to mention the
alphabet and did
find it even though
my name was not used

perception perception
to know me so well
before knowing me
and when i was young
as you and also
did not know me

VIII

a lot of body hair
has gone
            rubbed off
by furies i suppose

hundreds of them
all these years

IX

the heat rises
in us also

X

one would-be customer
complained to the local precinct
about his black eye
broken nose missing teeth

told police he went to the mansion
for oral sex went into
the wrong room and was beaten

XI

were you really
a model once

i was featured
in a movie

XII

a fool always a fool
for young women
                    when
young a young fool

now a middle-aged and
soon to be an old one

before they had
to be crazy and young
now they need be young only

and where before
they said it was because
i was a poet
                    now it's because
they have this hang-up see
about older men

XIII

she was perfect still
though twenty years
later
    and she undressed
so quickly yes too
quickly
      perfect
she undressed

XIV

at last i understand
the young
              are for
the young

you will never warm
these bones with
that flesh
              that flesh
will warm bones
that need no warming

oh you will come
because i need never
because you want

also i will watch
as he watches
you and see his
face light as
mine stays dark

at last i
understand this

XV

cleanliness is next
to godliness especially
this once in twenty-eight
years easter and pesach
coincide and so
i do my laundry

there is a note
on the bulletin board

whoever has my blue genes
please return them

To arrive at the simplest truth . . . .
requires years of contemplation.
Not activity.
Not reasoning.
Not calculating.
Not busy behavior of any kind.
Not reading.
Not talking.
Not making an effort.
Not thinking.
Simple bearing in mind what it is one needs to know.

from Laws of Form/G Spencer Brown

I

you smell good she
said like in eighth grade

followed by stories
of her grandpa
and the skunks

how to take that

II

rain
    breasts
        new pink dress
allowed only the first i
imagine april in your letter

III

strange winter with
spring before
groundhog day and
warm rain then
and dropping tonight
and back to winter

but he will not
see his shadow while
it rains

and spring will come
quickly then

time to oil up
the baseball glove
and get the arm
back in shape

IV

in the seat
of a car
like teenagers

grandson asleep
in the house
twelve feet away
dreaming of mother's
nipples and milk
sweet and warm

what were we
dreaming of

V

spent the night
talking who is
your favorite writer
deja vu of thirty
years ago and not since

good list for prose
but the poets left
something to be desired

which was the point
to leave something
to be desired ah

to bed alone both poets
both desiring both
waiting for it yet

VI

we open like flowers
and then we discover
why the rose has thorns

VII

trying to explain
to a blonde who lives
with somebody else
and a waitress
i hardly know
they both look summery
which they take to mean
they are unclothed

of course but to explain
i can see breasts any time
but shoulders bared
in the streets and
in public restaurants
only in summer and
i like it summery

they think i want their bodies
and don't know how it eases me
simply to see their shoulders

the last b'rucha of
the two hundred and sixteen
says thanks for the making
of beauty on this earth

VIII

at my age she said i
am tired of men who are
still working out their
anger against mother

i said let it
serve notice

IX

summers are
full of love
for us

winters
we are old men

X

some women having let
their body hair grow
are then disturbed to find
their husbands find it erotic
when that was not the point

XI

a postcard from nice
la promenade des anglais
obviously a french joke
since les anglais
don't go bare-breasted
yet inset bare-breasted
maiden large straw hat
shading her eyes and
one hand holding it
brown nipples atilt

dear joel it's true
on every beach
you never know
where to look
not good form
to be caught gaping
unfortunately
what we've always
known is true
the ideal tits
are in our heads
but then one set
comes by and

and he is a painter
and he ought to know

XII

have stick will
travel says
the journeyman printer
knowing the journey
really means working
day by day you
don't own the shop
and stay there
all the days

it's not taking
a trip not
necessarily moving
in so cumbered
is a good word
angel woman
alas in chicago
while i do
my day's work
un incumbered here
in new york

XIII

it is two days since
the lady said i am
comfortable but cautious
as i kissed her full
soft cold lips to
no response and it is
three days since the
lady couldn't dance
because of sciatica
and four days past
the lady who didn't
answer her phone

XIV

three years later
live cigar in my hand
she asked are you
still smoking

inhaled and said
no but i moved
the catbox

now it dosen't
stink up the kitchen
it wouldn't offend
you any more

the same round
breasts and face
three years later
but like miss crab
said to mr lobster
after learning
to walk frontwards

would you please
get out of my way

XV

aphrodite
she says last night
she read my words
while rude boys called

for meat she said
they want just meat
to ease themselves
and not her self

o she is wrong
beautiful one
they want only
you
    i also

and sometimes meat
body calling
other bodies

sometimes as more

yes
    love us all
as we love you
or let us be
needless
        alone

the more laws and restrictions
the poorer the people

the sharper the weapons
the more trouble

the more ingenious and clever
the more strange things happen

the more rules and regulations
the more thieves and robbers . . . .

from The Way and The Power/Lao Tse

I

xeng-li the name
means success the sex
not definitely known
but thought to be male
the child of pe-pe and yin-yin
born in a zoo in mexico city

an international storm the
director of the washington
zoo mexico has lucked out
completely their pandas are young
and just barely sexually mature
and everything must have happened
at just the right time
and they must have liked each other

it is hard to find compatible pandas'

II

to you i was always an enemy
you were always an enemy to me

but they look at us
and see no difference
we are all enemies to them

and they to us of course

III
despite my
own labors
and the kids
there was
a mouse in
nat's waste
basket a
triumph again
of nature
over art

IV

seeking seeking a new discipline
on which to base their careers
two psychiatrists look at the artwork

a sculpture two thousand years old
from the shaft tombs of western mexico
shows a woman just after giving birth

they say she is suffering from
classic post-partum depression

we know from history later on
aztec midwives tried to stop these blues
by assuring new mothers they'd behaved
like the eagle and the tiger
and had won a real battle
just like the bravest soldiers

in four other figures they say they see
cases of true or clinical depression
as distinguished from simple grief or madness
and presumably also post-partum depression

and another is taciturn gloomy despondent
which is yet another image of the same they say

a thousand years later late classic maya
shows them an old woman biting her nails
and they say this typifies yet another
state of agitated depression which often
accompanies advancing age even today i say
while another elderly man from this period
has a bland expression drooping lip
and is presumed silent which they say
are also characteristics of ditto
and in fact to them the figure's stare
recalls galen's description of
the melancholic state dread and desire
death both at the same time

galen also lived a long time ago
but not as long ago as some old people
although longer ago than the shrinkers

anyhow all these old statues cause them
to conclude these peoples recognized
dementia and other psychoses and there
is of course ample proof that the aztecs
conferred with the spanish about at least two
forms of depression after losing to them
the question is mostly are all
psychiatrists fools or only these

of course our ancestors bit their
nails at walls and stayed
silent impressed by the act of
giving birth to another or the
equally impressive act of aging

they too got depressed and galen too

and god knows i do reading
these tedious theories forced
into life to bolster their jobs and
stop their fingernail biting which
led them into psychiatry in the
first place
                better to stare at walls
but they'll never discover that

V

weeds are a purely
arbitrary designation
saying hey you you're
a weed you're not
a flower as if they were
some separate species

i prefer the german
way of looking at it
unkraut no cabbage

if you can't eat it
and you can't paint
it then fuck it and
if you can't even do
that you might as
well salute it the
gi's used to say

VI

seven-thirty in the morning
couple in shiny english boots
whipcord jodhpurs riding caps
blue broadcloth shirts whips
walking down hudson there
are no stables that way

VII

the vegetarian piranha
live on fruits and seeds

large molars and muscled jaws
let them crack hard nuts
in the flood plains of brazil
among the watery forests

the fish then shit the seeds
and the trees are born again

in rapid succession you'll hear
a pop when the pods explode to
scatter the seeds and a plop
when a seed hits the water and
a gulp when the fish swallows it

if you cut down the trees
you're bound to decrease the catch

VIII

they set up headquarters
registered the prospectors
declared the site closed
to any others
vaccinated the colony
against yellow fever and meningitis
banned women and alcohol
announced that anyone
firing a weapon
would be expelled
set up a loudspeaker
to play country music
during off hours
and the national anthem
at morning and evening
flag raising and lowering

each night soft-core
pornographic films
are shown on the airstrip

IX

the soviets have opened war
on the villages of afghanistan
students businessmen professionals
commute to battle next
to moslem holy warriors

X

the leader of the basques
fighting for autonomy
says no political entity
can live without a
coercive apparatus

i am reading this
two days after the anniversary
of the fall of the bastille

presumably that coercive apparatus
is what we have all been fighting for

XI

surely in buffalo
there's one bar
where they want us
to come and sit
and talk all night
just a bar to talk

XII

eleven years ago
i stopped making love
to watch cleon jones
put the team ahead
in a crucial game

stopped the act of love
to watch baseball
on television
a ballclub in
a pennant race

not important except
to remember committing
this act life vs art
art vs art culture vs
the individual whatever

eleven years later
there is always something
embarassing to remember
something we did that was
shameful ridiculous and
shameful something
to wish undone

but that marriage is gone
and the team won the pennant

XIII

and here's your checklist
for mother's day

heinz beans
del monte tomato sauce
ronzoni spaghetti
aqua-fresh toothpaste
minute maid orange juice
dellwood low fat milk
temtee whipped cream cheese
pepsi cola
lipman chickens
boneless london broil
boneless turkey cutlets
ground chuck
fresh salads
lean boiled deli ham

most stores open sunday

XIV

each day
is one day gone
and you should not
understand this

you are not fifty

XV

devil kissed me

saw cathedral
                 but in plan
not real

.

Our life today is poisoned to the root. Man has ousted the beasts and trees, has poisoned the air, and filled up the open spaces. Worse things may happen. That melancholy and industrious animal -- man -- may discover new forces and harness them to his chariot. Some such danger is in the air. The result will be a great abundance -- of human beings! Every square yard will be occupied by a man. Who will be able then to cure us of the lack of air and space? The mere thought of it suffocates me.

But it is not only that, not only that. Every effort to procure health is in vain. Health can only belong to the beasts, whose sole idea of progress is in their own bodies ... spectacled man invents instruments outside his body, and if there was any health or nobility in the inventor there is none in the user. Implements are bought or sold or stolen, and man goes on getting weaker and more cunning. It is natural that his cunning should increase in proportion to his weakness. The earliest implements only added to the length of his arm, and could not be employed except by the exercise of his own strength. But a machine bears no relationship to the body. The machine creates disease because it denies what has been the law of creation throughout the ages. The law of the strongest disappeared, and we have abandoned natural selection. We need something more than psychoanalysis to help us.

Under the law of the greatest number of machines, disease will prosper and the diseased will grow ever more numerous.

Perhaps some incredible disaster produced by machines will lead us back to health.

When all the poison gases are exhausted, a man, made like all other men of flesh and blood, will in the quiet of his room invent an explosive of such potency that all the explosives in existence will seem like harmless toys beside it. And another man, made in his image, and in the image of all the rest, but a little weaker than them, will steal that explosive and crawl to the center of the earth with it, and place it just where he calculates it would have the maximum effect. There will be a tremendous explosion, but no one will hear it and the earth will return to its nebulous state and go wandering through the sky, free at last from parasities and disease.

from Confessions of Zeno/Italo Svevo

I

bewildered in the
morning heat
i take an apricot
i take a plum

though they taste
good to me only
the first bite
is accurate in
what we expect

finally they cloy
too much or not
enough of what
we eternally desire

nothing is ever
perfect in this world

one bite is perfect
still it leads
to another

II

in albuquerque
they want bridges
over the rio grande
to save time

they will wreck
the centuries old
irrigation system

they want
even more cars
they will block
the whooping cranes
who fly over
they are already
blanketed by
pollution every winter

but rush hour
has worsened

the fight is
over technicalities

at the northern tip
of the unbridged stretch
is one of the last stands
of primitive cottonwoods

the last stand

III

seeing the woman
corner of bleecker and bank
paper in hand blank look
asking for help

where are you going

whither goest thou

wanted west broadway
castelli gallery
you're a far piece
she was just that
since she was swedish

it's a walk if you don't mind
she smiled no are you maybe
walking also that way
no i go this but
if you stay on bleecker
long enough you'll

crazy walking by interjected
go straight to hell
you know i said
he's right follow bleecker
down to la guardia
go right past houston
you'll get there
gallery or hell

left her smiling swedish

IV

amenophis III
akhenaten
smenkhkare
and tutankhamen
's mummy cases
show them with
female breasts

the doctor says
these were real
the result of
hereditary
pseudohermaphroditism
so common in families
with a long history of incest

pharaohs of the eighteenth dynasty
commonly married their sisters
daughters and other close relatives

and oedipus as we know
across the mediterranean
went blind because
he was a bad mother fucker

V

the topic sentence says
by any rational calculation
the potential benefits
vastly outweigh potential costs

the first major point is
suppose one or more
great oil spills blight the region

it is answered that
the economic loss would be great
but not greater than the losses
from the eruption of mt st helens
or the droughts that strike
the grain belt every decade or two

the second major point is
the ecological damage
would also be terrible

it is answered that it would not be
more terrible than the damage
inflicted on the deserts of the southwest
by poor land-use planning

the third major point states that
those who prefer to go slow
note that the oil would not disappear
if it were left in place for another decade

and this is answered that
unfortunately the timing of the flow
could be critical to economic stability

so in summing up it says
every effort should be made
to exploit the alaskan oil reserve
with minimal environmental damage
but whatever the valid hesitations
they should not be allowed
to cloud our economic future

to which the teacher comments that the
rhyme interjected into the last
clause of allowed and cloud is
distracting and unfortunate
and that our economic future has
been clouded anyway since the
industrial revolution began
since man began
to eat himself

VI

he rings the bell
for his friend
at five of eight
this morning
his towel and
bathing suit
slung over shoulder

it is the fourth hot day

she comes by and tells me
harry is dead

she wants to discuss
the fact that he kept
taking himself out
of the hospital
wouldn't stay in
and now is dead

she says he was
too young to die

all people die too young
but could a hospital
have helped him

but i cannot debate this now
since these kids are ready
and i must pay attention
to their needs

always when someone dies
there are kids eight and ten
needing attention

even when homer and chaucer died
and when i die also

so we go downstairs
to meet the bus
so then they can swim
this hot day

while harry's grave waits
at another end of the city

VII

wrestled to the ground
like jacob or the angel
hogtied by six presby
terian ministers all
i wanted was my damned
breakfast they were
visiting the college
for a one-day program
in handling stress i
figured they wanted
to see how much they
could put me under

while we talked
about god and secular
humanism i
took to staring out
the windows and saw
how the lake'd been
lowered for winter
so the weeds would
die the larvae too
to benefit next
summer's season

it was a man-made
lake in which now
the stumps and all
the bric-a-brac
showed with water
only toe-deep

i said well at
least this here's
a great place now for
walking on the waters

and finished off my
breakfast in the peace
that passeth understanding

VIII

teachers dissatisfied
world fertility in
rapid decline what
are those lights
on the moon

IX

belltower's computer
tells seasons

i see orion
high in night sky

X

ciba-geigy corp

glens falls

general electric

hudson falls

chase bag company
general electric

fort edward

scott paper company

schuylerville
stillwater
mechanicville

general electric
park guilderland sewage treatment plant

troy

al tech specialty steel corporation
bendix corporation
ford motor company

albany north wastewater treatment plant
rensselaer county sewer district

rensselaer

chemical leaman tank lines
ashland chemical company

albany

albany south wastewater treatment plant
albany steam station
consolidated rail corporation
general electric
lion brand corporation

catskill

alpha portland cement
dutchess metal finishes

kingston

hercules incorporated
culligan water conditioning
western publishing
ibm

poughkeepsie

poughkeepsie water treatment plant
central hudson gas and electric
new york trap rock
three star anodizing
ibm

beacon

montgomery worsted mills

newburgh

texaco
tuck industries
marathon battery
majestic weaving company incorporated
consolidated edison

peekskill

state power authority
orange and rockland utilities
u s gypsum
lightron corporation
orange and rockland utilities

tarrytown

federal paper board
glenshaw glass
anaconda wire and cable division
phelps dodge wire and cable company
town of west new york
city of new york
city of hoboken
jersey city sewage authority

jersey city
newark

new york city

and the 'american
rhine' flows thus
unbroken to the sea

thalassa! thalassa!

XI

you can write anything
someone will listen and applaud
but to write something
and to listen yourself
and still applaud

XII

or to arrive at a place
and say this is the place
that kills

of course the people
but the place also

and to wake there alone

XIII

brewing plant compounds
in the kitchen
is not everyone's
cup of tea

many american and
european women
would rather take a pill
because it seems
more scientific

they are trying
to isolate
the secret ingredient
of this herbal
birth control
so it can be
duplicated in
the laboratory'

the beauty
is its simplicity

it is common
and found in many
parts of the world

all a woman has to do
is sip the bitter
herbal tea the morning
after sex and her
worries will be over

but a pill seems
more scientific

but they will be
silent until the
experiments are
completed

women will be able
to grow and gather it
and make their tea

but a pill seems
more scientific

of course a needle would
be even more so
but a pill is the
middle road no

and mum is the word
and mom is a word too
and so is apple pie
with the bitter tea
every morning when
the experiments
are complete

XIV

mao sd
there is no
occident

XV

others have said it
and i repeat i repeat

Pain and love -- the whole of life, in short -- cannot be looked on as a disease just because they make us suffer.

from Confessions of Zeno/Italo Svevo